This book is dedicated to my wife,
Carol,
who has been my support, my comfort,
and my love,
through all of the years I have known her.

THE COLOURS OF THE EARTH

from **1914**
Sonnet IV, *The Dead*

by Rupert Brooke

These hearts were woven of human joys and cares,
   Washed marvellously with sorrow, swift to mirth.
The years had given them kindness. Dawn was theirs,
   And sunset, and the colours of the earth.
These had seen movement, and heard music, known
   Slumber and waking; loved; gone proudly friended;
Felt the quick stir of wonder; sat alone;
   Touched flowers and furs and cheeks. All this is ended.

There are waters blown by changing winds to laughter
   And lit by the rich skies, all day. And after,
Frost, with a gesture, stays the waves that dance
   And wandering loveliness. He leaves a white
Unbroken glory, a gathered radiance,
   A width, a shining peace, under the night.

© Michael W. Lemberger

Table of Contents

People

B. 19 SEPTEMBER

Flutter of blossoms
Gentle wave of grain
Rustle of green leaves
Aromas fill the air

Just as sensory pleasures come
So we know the presence
Of our friend
Provides this same effect
This pleasant point of view

A graciousness exudes
Surrounds the circle
Encompasses her world
Found worthy of the gleam
That pours from stars

This friendship treasured most
For auras brought to bear
Against the sterner sides
Made mellow by her worth

C. 11 MARCH

To whom brevity
is a virtue.
Yet standing
like sturdy buttress
for worthy largess
on all those granite walls
of each Medieval
cathedral.

Generous
where expression
of need
challenges the mind.

Treasure
wrapped in tapestry.

FOR HARVEY, AT 90

Roots in Iowa soil
Full growth
        on Missouri River flood plain
Maturity in that thin air
        by the Great Stoney Front
A cycle has evolved
To bring us to this day

Seams cut deeply
Formed on myriad Pacific atolls
Carrying the flag
To higher honors

Gentle, flowing years
Matched by swelling love
Harvest of a lifetime
Spent in keen support

Now gathered in with joy

J. 25 AUGUST

Earth and sky
Fire and water
Elements that form
Life's basic core
They meet in joyous union

A flowering of the time
When mind and tongue
Seem sharply lilting
Marching to the step
Of unseen drums
Yet living in creation
Made whole by love of friends
And love of God

Images
Delightful in their scope
Meeting in the light -
The charm -
Of this beloved friend

K. 15 AUGUST

Flowering trees
encouraging thoughts

Blossoming shrubs
embracing days

Views of cotton clouds
floating past the horizon

Sparkling showers of rain
merged with misty dew

Fenced by clipped yew
in formal rows

A casual stroll
along the graveled paths
of Karyn's garden
allows our eyes the treat
of softest pinks
and brightest reds

Colors all enhanced
by sunlight glow

L. 8 JULY

A woman named Laura
Or - should it be
A woman "called" Laura
Images come to mind
Conjured up
As echoes from the past
Or kismet yet to come

For some
A sentimental song
Words of Johnny Mercer
Notes of David Raksin
A movie for the heart
For others
A sad heroine
Preoccupied
With glass menagerie

All these things
Come upon our mind
But fail to sweep away
Recognition of our friend
No besom clears the way
So we are left
With spirit and with kind
This meeting of the thoughts
That let us welcome back
A friend named Laura

N. 22 FEBRUARY

We know her
as we know
what is right,
nay, righteous,
in our lives.
A woman of stature
in every sense
of that effective word.

Clouds scud quickly
across the silken sky;
bringing hope
and promise
of what will bc.

No idiosyncratic thoughts
become ideals;
and yet
we find the truths --
guideposts for our minds.

Nature

AUTUMN THOUGHTS

Days of clouds and rain
Gloom hovers around
Grey veil stretches across
The narrowing sky
Fallen leaves lie soggy
Impacted into damp masses

October crouches low
In preparation for the leap
Into December winter

The world turns inward
Anticipates snow blanketing
Hibernation until Spring

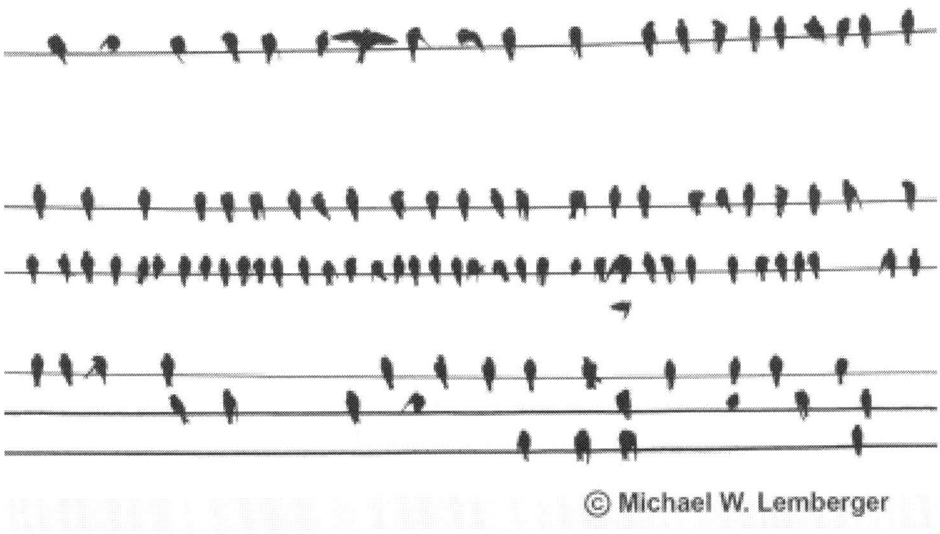

BIRDS ON A WIRE

What does it most remind us of,
That row of birds along the utility wire;
Requiring neither pole nor tree nor map
To distribute themselves quite evenly?

In space, drill, symmetrical pattern,
Might it be a solemn, robed procession,
Of choir boys in Salisbury Cathedral.
So perfectly aligned in choir stalls?

Or is it rather some heroic event,
Bringing forth the soldiers, rank on rank,
Shoulder to shoulder, making a straight facade?

The birds may be of species this or that,
Since distance makes the shapes so indistinct.
Their songs are but an echo to our ears;
It is our eyes they take possession of.

COLORS

A cardinal
painfully red
perched on a branch
startling against greyish green
of cedar tree
with caps of snow
framing his silhouette

An oriental poppy
huddled at garden's edge
fragile petals
so brilliantly orange
reminiscent of the silken robe
worn by emperors in Cathay

Other hues emerge
so delicately shy
as if fearing to assert
their rightful place
in the rainbow spectrum

A banquet for the eye
induces euphoria
surfeit of joy

Loren N. Horton

DECEMBER WEATHER

Snowfall glitters
Starlight glimmers
Points of brilliant light
Shimmer on the glaze
Of ice-bound streams

Stillness hovers
Hushing the fluttering flakes
To mute repose
Across the sheeted earth

Calm enfolds the scene
As branch and twig and bush
Keep silence
In the light and in the dark
While snowflakes fall

IT'S STILL WINTER

Snow, snow, snow
Piles, drifts, carpets
Cover the dozing earth
Disguise harvest waste
Hold down wadded leaves

Winds chill the days
Coupled to keening winds
Winter comes and stays
Smothering sight and smell
Until the touch of thaw

DIALOGUE

Palm tree
Dripping fronds

Dates suspended
In abundant richness

Roughened trunk
Providing handholds
For man and monkey

Oak tree
Dropping acorns

Bronze leaves
Burnished by fall sunlight
Later to join
Matted timber loam
To generate new growth

EARLY SPRING

How refreshing!
The pianissimo wind
Which warms the day

It breaks the grip of winter
And opens the curtains
To disrobed trees
Rapidly clothed in foliage
Easing the view
Accustomed more to snow
And earthy tones

Our thanks to all the signs
Of early Spring

EVENING CLOUDS

Scattered wisps
of purplish clouds
frolic in abandon,
much like chaff and straw
caught in summer breeze
at threshing time.

Haze playfully skips
through silhouettes
of leafless trees,
standing at parade rest
across the prospect,
stretched to limitless lengths.

EVENING FOG

Tendrils of fog
Snake their way
Through routes obscured
By stones and trees and marsh

Grey wings curl
Under branches
Hung heavily with mist
Creating a knitted framework
Of muted fabric

Moist threads
Form filaments
Which trail, indistinct,
Until thcy fade away

No little cat feet
This slinking mass

GREEN AND BROWN

A pond

Cattail reeds
Emerge from water
Waterlily leaves
Float on water

Monet paintings
Impressionist beauty
In nature

In decorator shops
Arranged in vases and bowls
Soothing contrasts
Of green and brown
Mirrored in thoughtful eyes

Present in spring
Brightest in summer
Decayed in fall
Reeds and leaves
Nature's cycle

A JOURNEY

Begin at a stone in a public road
A fingerpost will give the certain clue
About directions to be followed

Mind the grassy verge and ditch
Skirt the hedge and woodland copse

Enjoy the fragmentary sunlight
Sometimes slipping through the leaves
Of trees which overhang the path

Inhale the scent of border primroses
Casual west winds may caress
As they continue on their chosen way
Cooling the farm hands in nearby fields
While fanning stems and grass and leaves

Gentle hills and slopes combine
To ease the passage of these tired feet
Until the journey ends in greying dusk
And all the world is given up to ease

LOESS HILLS

Dawn breaks
Over the edge of Loess Hills
Views of sunset
Appear
Across the Missouri flood plain

Vast remnants
From glacial meltwater
Rushing south
Drying into particles
Lifted by prevailing winds
Dumped in ignominious heaps
There to endure
For millennia
Finally emerging
As this chain of bluffs
Bald-pated hills
Vegetation sparse
Habitat for curious species
Plants, butterflies, mammals
Out of character
In these northern regions
Skippers flutter
From yucca to lead plant

Created Eden
Feast for human eyes
Banquet for human spirit

A NEW LOOK AT SPRING

A sense of wonder
Permeates the air

A certain sense of wonder
Dominates my mind

Look around and see
If there be any sight
More marvelous than this
The first appearance
Of daffodils and grass
Emerging from their rest
To burst forth in a glory
Of such a pleasant Spring

NIGHT HAWKS

Night hawks dart
With abandon

Across the rooftops
Over the wires
In pairs

Plunge briskly
Sheer off
At the last moment

Veering towards trees
Soaring aloft

Choreography
Of nature's aerial dance

NATURE'S CYCLE

once living tree
now dead
outlined against the sky
in feeble remnant
of former glory
raising its skeletal hand
in supplication
to unknown deities
stark against sunlight
barren residue

THE OSAGE ORANGE HEDGE

It was a fence
Across the east field
Of the farm
Planted in optimism
Grown in seasons
That passed
War, depression, war
Trimmed properly
It served its purpose well
Hog tight
Horse high
Bull strong
Its dense, green shoots
Intertwined like lace
An intricate basket weave
Producing a fruit
Sometimes called hedge balls
Other times called hedge apples
Rounded, indented surfaces
Like a human brain
Rendered in light green
These knarled and twisted
Branches and sprouts
Long a common feature
Of rural countryside
Made obsolete
By barbed wire, woven wire
Now a victim
Of technological progress
Remnants left
Reminders of a past
When usefulness
Combined with beauty
Nightmarish future
Someday to fall
Uprooted and jumbled
By bulldozer blade
Leaving only the wounded earth
To spur memories

Loren N. Horton

REMEMBERING

Robert Frost wrote
about the road less traveled
he also wrote
about a snowy evening
Frost's New England eyes
recognized the beauty
of winter travel
when ice coats the branches
of adjacent trees

and snow piles up
on red cedar branches
much like the epaulets
on shoulders of Latin American colonels

snow and ice
conceal a dingy view
of roads turned dreary
until the warming spring

SEA SCENES

I have seen the gulls
        circling
I have watched the gulls
        swooping
Gull's wings
Like fluffy boomerangs
Flattened across the sky
Only interrupted
        by nimbus clouds
        and a sailing wind

Gulls finally coming to rest
Sitting peaceably
On the rotted posts
Remaining from cypress dock

Gulls milling about
Restless in their search
        for the next meal
        or a present snack

Gulls preening their feathers
Unaware
Of my constant gaze

Loren N. Horton

A SENSE OF SPRING

All senses bright and clear
We like the smells of Spring
Flowers, leaves, remains of leaf mould
The smells are mixed with sights
So welcome after winter scenes
Sounds of southern winds
Combine with ear and touch

Our minds absorb with ease
Our feelings merge in joy
These are the marks of Spring

SHAGBARK HICKORY

under the gnarled roots
beneath the strips and fragments of bark
beside the leaf mould
        now grown compact
        with passing seasons
there comes a hidden stimulus
when the kernels break their shells
and burst into fertile life
in springtime
        burgeoning with growth
sometime to replace
the awesome grandeur
of the parent tree
in timbered companionship

nature's resurrection

RIVER BLUFFS

limestone ledges
centuries of weathering
by water and wind
striations brutally evident
variegated shades
from grey to brown to white
lying in unfinished shelves
awaiting new-bought goods
cavities gaping here and there
rock shelters for early families
needing shelter from winter wind
and cover from snow and rain

hawks circle slowly
on search for prey
eagles dive swiftly
at fish in the river far below
turkey vultures rise on thermals
song birds chatter in nearby trees
cicadas chirp in deepening dusk
light green willow shoots
thrust their points out of sand bars
cottonwood leaves rustle in light breeze
scenes of pastoral tranquillity
that rest beneath the sharp-faced bluffs

capturing artistic attention
drawing perspective eyes
producing uncompleted sketches
good angles for photographs
right degree of shadow
balanced with filtered sunlight

limestone ledges
matured through freeze and thaw
another masterpiece of nature
unpolished geological presentation
through measures of horizontal strength
impressive in terms of simple mass
these uneven parallel lines of rock
markers for the pages of time

SIGNS OF SPRING # 1

gently
the delicate tips of grass
expose such newness
now freshly born
from dank earth

soon to shoot
towards the nurturing sun
with grace
and elegance

SIGNS OF SPRING # 2

origins
in bulbs and buds
a metamorphosis
to new forms

those splashes of color
which spot the timber floor
reflections
of fallen rainbows

a feast for human eyes

SIGNS OF SPRING # 3

quietly
the breeze caresses
freshly budded limbs
of plum trees

softly
the breeze touches
surfaces of earth

scents of flowers
cover the fields

SIGNS OF SPRING # 4

brighter
shows the mid-day sun
filtered through the curtains
of meager clouds

warmer
shines the vernal light
fondling the sprouting plants

the world strengthens
its reborn life

THE SLOUGH

There is a time
In memory, dimmed by age
When we sometimes recall
That slough in the pasture
Where coarse grasses grow
Where red-winged blackbirds nest
Where dragonflies dart
In an aimless aerial dance
That has its own form

Summer winds stir the yellowing blades
In a symphony of constant grace
On occasion, some water puddles
Hidden in the shadowed hollows
Until they turn brown with seep
From last season's growth

Glad memories of former days

Loren N. Horton

SPRING GARDENS

Apologies to William Wordsworth

Daffodils

No field of golden daffodils
To greet the wandering eye
No passing of the whiter clouds
Obscuring domes of sky
But grey the slanting drops of rain
That damps the yearning face
So turned towards the stretching fields
Which overwhelm this place
So rest you easy, daffodils
My comrades of the later spring
Ensuing blossoms scent the air
All harbingers the light to bring
Your sunny contrast charms the mind
It whiles away the thoughts and time
Which linger more in greener days
Both flowers and grass in rhyme

Again we'll wait the coming spring
Those golden daffodils to bring

Tulips

Majestic blooms
Which rise from earthy bulbs
Emerge in blaze of colors
Wrestling for our attention
As we note the slender stalks
Nestled in beds of leaves

Offering cups of wine
Fermented not from grapes
But gentle blending
Of mind and eye
Harbingers of things to come
In that wonder that is Spring

A Red Tulip

Earlier this week
I noticed the first red tulip

It is early in the season
For tulips to bloom
Of course the daffodils
Are showing their pride
All over town
But tulips are a May flower
At least that is when
All the Tulip Festivals are held

It pleases my eye
To see a red tulip
Blooming in a front garden

Sure sign of Spring

Lilacs

Lilacs bloom
Early this year
Still April
Already
Purple flowers abound

Weigh down the branches
On myriad bushes

Scent and sight
Ornament the yards
Delight us
As we pass

White lilacs join their kin
Present delight
Early in the season

Peonies

Daffodils, tulips. lilacs
What will be next ?

Bulbous peonies
Forecast the coming flowers
Hanging so heavily
Over elliptic leaves

Favorite blossoms
For decorating graves
On May 30 each year

Pink, white, red
Peonies bring out
The glory of any bouquet

Iris

lovely iris
inspiration for Tennyson
revered by French royalty
commonly standing at attention
used as colorful borders
their sword-leaves dueling
in fresh Spring gales
fencing with their neighbors
defending their space
warding off intruder growth
of other Spring flowers

vivid purple hue
contrasts brightly
with sunny yellow
gentle lavender
or paler, creamy white

it makes a finer season
when enhanced
by crowds of iris

Snowball Bush

Cascades of blooms
Waterfalls of blossoms

Snowballs cluster
        on delicate branches
Visions of avalanches and glaciers

Wondrous sights
And glorious views
Verburnum species
        bloom in Spring
Hydrangea species
        bloom in Summer

Another beauty
Of the green season

Bridal Wreath

Aptly named
We see it with delight
Its tendrils droop
In graceful veils

Alternating strands
Suffused with green
Sprays of snowy flowers
Comforting masses
That seem to create
A waterfall of Spring

A Bed of Flowers

we might have found
pirate's treasure chest
shiny with gold and silver
not buried
on some deserted, tropical island

rather, confined
within disciplined herbaceous borders
colors sprung to life
in dozens of brilliant blooms
sparkling bright
in slanting sunlight
of drizzling rain

this English garden

Leaves

green leaves
explode in masses
obscure the bare branches
left over
from winter's chill

green leaves exposed
in bewildering variety
of shapes and sizes
form their own curtain
drawn to introduce
dramatic effects
of nature's work

SPRING TRIUMPHANT

shadows of mauve and grey
rest quietly in secret corners
awaiting the vernal equinox
which unlocks the rays of light
and unleashes the warming wind

shadows brighten imperceptibly
as colors move to green and gold
and the edges of the earth move back
to include encompassing views

then every eye begins to sparkle
with the delight and joy of Spring

TIMBERED RIDGE

Behold ! The white-veiled hills and slopes
    The stark and barren trees
    Free-born Roman sentinels
    Standing at attention
    As they populate the ridge
    Extending northward
    In a heavily timbered spur

Scattered patches of old snow
Huddle between and among
Myriad hickory saplings
And full-growth oaks

Sunlight penetrates
The densely woven branches
Now latticed across the tops
Making cross-hatched patterns
Of welcome brightness

TROUT STREAM

streams of water
rush along their course

glassy surfaces
are cracked in a thousand places
into fragmented prisms
which cast miniature rainbows
back at the primal sun

the heat of sky
the dark of night
the western wind
all bend the stone-filled slope
into a single sight

restless streams
these waters fed from snow
far above the understanding
of casual eyes

WINTER

Winter solstice sky
Winter solstice moon
Winter solstice wind

Blue bands streak the land
Dispersing warmer colors
While darkness creeps behind
As a curtain for the lighted sky

The black, the grey, the blue
Replace the green, brown, and bronze

Cold breath matches chill breeze
Stillness surrounds the earth
And nature pauses in rest

Photo by Michael W. Lemberger

WINTER SCENE

soft, gentle snow
falls slowly
coating branch and bush
in pillowed piles

a north wind
brushes fallen snow
into crusty drifts
like ivory walls

Faith

GIFTS FROM GOD

Unseemly brightness
Brilliance of the highest sun
Rays and beams
Permeating skin and thought
Radiance focused
On people, on earth
Unreflected from the fields
Absorbed directly into soil
Warming seed and root
Benefitting gentle growth
Glorious light
Direct from sun to earth
Gift from God

GOD'S CARE

God's blessings -
Continuous in joy
They bring to all our lives
Blessings spread
Throughout all lands and seas
In wondrous comfort
To everyone

Days merge to years
As hours merge to days
Content in knowing
The strengths of God's Care

Loren N. Horton

THE HOLY IN THE ORDINARY

A seed planted in a furrow
A farmer watching hopefully for rain
A sprout inserted into tilled soil
A gardener weeding with loving care
A full blown rose catching the morning dew
A florist carefully pruning a bush

Cause and effect

Cause and effect

Eternal cycle of the seasons
Plow, plant, cultivate
Enjoy the riches of the harvest

Cause and effect

Sunrise, sunset
Spring, summer, fall
Grow, growing, growth
Emerging bud, gently curling leaf
Dawn, darkness
Birth, death
The going out, the coming in

Cause and effect

Transitions in mind and body
Hours, days, years
Plain wrapping on the rarest gifts
The Holy in the Ordinary

CANTICLE FOR EVERLASTING LIFE

Canticle for everlasting life
This life that knows no end
Resolutions by God's will
Discernment by the mind
From birth through death
Into darkness of night
Then brightness of day
Songs of praise
Psalms of joy
Merged as the river and the sea
In glorious eternity

THE MANY VOICES OF GOD

What voice is this
We hear

In the clap of thunder
In the crash of lightning

In the wailing wind
Whistling across the sky
Bending the young trees

In the murmur
Of mountain streams
Gurgling over ancient stones

In the faintest roar
Of far off waterfalls

In the cheerful songs
Of birds that perch
On branches of the swaying
maple

In the scuttering
Of rabbits' feet
As they scurry about
The grassy fields

In the pounding rush
Of spring rains
Watering the fields
With life-giving moisture

All these voices
We hear in night and day
We hear in all the seasons
We hear with ears attuned
As we see with eyes alight
All senses brought to life
By the heavenly sounds
Of God's own voice
Bringing us to calm
And peace
Within our busy lives
Soothing all turmoil

Gesturing us to rest
From our waking
To our sleeping
By day
And in our lives

God's light shines through
The deepest darkness
God's sound penetrates
The closest stillness

The voice we hear
Is God's own voice
Coming to us
In all the sounds
Of nature

OUR MIGHTY GOD

God resides in the high places
All powerful, omnipresent
God is present in the waters
Almighty, omniscient
Holy places abound
Where God is ever with us
Praise God in His goodness
Worship God in His holiness
Glory shines on all the earth
Reflection of our mighty God

OUR NURTURING GOD

With gently fluttering snowfall
Soft piles accumulate
On bare branches of trees
Denuded for winter

Blessings from God
Descend to earth
They accumulate within
The better to help us

Our lives
No more seem barren
Thanks be to God
Our nurturing God

PATHS OF FAITH

In Gray's great *Elegy*
Paths of glory
Lead but to the grave

Paths of faith
Lead to God's own care
Of all those in need
Or lost in daily woe

Answers to our prayers
Restore our grieving souls
And build a strengthened faith

THE SHINING LIGHT OF GOD

The shining light of God
Blazes forth
    from sun
    from moon
    from stars
    from countenances of blessed
This shining light
    removes all shred of dark
    eliminates the shadows
    consoles the weak of heart
    comforts the grieving
Praise God in all things

Loren N. Horton

PATHS TO MIRIAM

A sisterhood
joined in bondage
to the Holy Will

Sarah, moved from Ur to Haran
Hagar, exiled to the desert
Rebekah, offering water to a stranger
Rachel, herding sheep
        though graceful and beautiful
Leah, resorting to primacy
Dinah, victimized
        by royal strength
        or by her own brothers
The cunning of Potiphar's wife
Abishag, sacrificed
        servant to the King
        perhaps the Rose of Sharon
        longing for her shepherd

Worth of Moses
        measured equally in Miriam, and Aaron
        soothsayers of the Lord
        no righteous retribution
        injustice manifested
        without recourse to appeal

England

AVEBURY

circle of megaliths
upright and sturdy
no dolmen
but individual stands
protected by earthen moat
and broad embankment
set amid fertile fields
on Salisbury Plain
no more in danger
of Nazi bombs
or selfish fellows
intent on grading
and building
to shape the land
for habitation
on a landscape
already altered
by human hands
in the creation
of this great circle

DRUIDS

Waving silver wands
Mumbled incantations
Mysterious potions
Worship from beyond
Remainder from lost times
Reminder of past days
Recall for the soul

Oak trees
Hill tops
Bonfires
Stretching over years
To this memory

DUDDEN DALE
(GREATER LANGDALE ROAD)

Tumbling, rumbling
        rounded boulders
Sweeping slopes
        blotches gently wafting down
        below the drifting clouds
Blotchy shadows wafting
Thundering, bounding, bouncing
        grumbling
Up and out and over and beyond
Down the fierce slopes
The chasms good and bold
Basso profunda
Unaligned with mirrors or with hope
That brilliant knife-edge
Slicing out the forms
Glissade
Cairn of memory
Cairn of longing
        to be with us still

© Michael W. Lemberger

COVENTRY CATHEDRAL

Ruins of medieval splendour
Still marked by fragile walls
Victims of Nazi air raids
The new cathedral
Rising phoenix-like
From the pile of rubble
Commemorating its predecessor
Much grandeur gone amiss
Destroyed by bombs and fire
Unlucky in its fate
A sister church in the south
Spire rising majestically from Salisbury Plain
Was spared this desecration
As were the monuments of London
Westminster Abbey and St. Paul's

The blitz of 1940
And the years of constant raids
Took their toll on sweeping stretches
Of the historic city
While in the countryside
Safety was a precious hope
Ended when the bombs dropped
On Coventry, and left a wreck
Of what had once been glorious

But Nazi air raids had effect
Though opposite of German aims
Resolve of people stiffened
And resistance and resolve
Became the very sinews
Of the ultimate victory

EAST ANGLIA

surging North Sea
rumbling ashore
in ever-crescendoing assault
icy breath of mist
fog laying coverlet heavy
chill winds
pealing off The Wash

solid dikes
canals and drainage ditches
gatekeepers' ghosts

sky-piercing spires
of myriad wool churches
sadly needing care

level land
water-logged and green
water meadows to the strand
fens and broads
pungent with salt water smell
lying vulnerable
defended feebly
by sand and shale and gorse
open to ravages
of storm and season

Loren N. Horton

GUNNER GILL

I plunge my hand
into the frigid water
of Gunner Gill
chortling down the fell
to join the Swale
I clutch a smallish stone
retrieve it from its fellows
feel the rounded contour
evened by years of flow
eroded into smoothness
I withdraw my hand
from the crackling surface
of Gunner Gill
I look upon my stone
to contemplate its sides
then think again
release the stone into clearness
that is the flow of Gunner Gill
My stone resumes its role
among its comrades
where it rests familiar
in its customary place
where days and months
of crisp water movement
keep it comfortable
I remove my hand
from Gunner Gill
content to leave the place
for all the future seasons
to contribute to the action
creating all the beauty
of Gunner Gill

LINES COMPOSED THOUSANDS OF MILES FROM TINTERN ABBEY

dragon fly
subject of Asian art
grasshopper
scourge of farm fields
cricket
sacred at sundown time

metallic gold beetles
hard-backed and shiny
inch worms
bunching their way
to destinations we do not know
tumblebugs
rolling their loads of dung
over clod and furrow

lest we forget
the ever-diligent ant
marching in columns
reminiscent of Roman legions
back and forth
from hills of excavated soil
with nary break nor vacation

ON FIRST SEEING THE WHITE CLIFFS OF DOVER

Mementoes carried far away
Where diaspora moves migrants
Certain landmarks stand alone
Traditions, events, and places
Bring one's homeland into focus

Eyes grown misted from memories
Mind still crowded with thoughts
Visual images matched with reality
Such expectations of this sight
First glimpse of history realized

An icon from two great wars
A simple phrase familiar to many
The song a comfort to saddened hearts
Who looked forward to bluebirds
Flying over those same white cliffs

The cliffs stand in sharpened contrast
To the thrashing waters at their feet
Waves and foam of the Channel sea
Sheer chalk faces rise in upward thrust
Marking the start of English land

Travellers sight the cliffs from boats
Sometimes from airplanes heading west
Hikers move carefully along the crest
Whether from the sea or air or land
Views of white cliffs mark their home

REMEMBERING OSCAR WILDE

A beatific glance
Such as might become
The prisoner
In Reading Gaol
Who cast a wistful eye
Towards the sky
Oscar knew that feeling
Though wit was blurred
By slings and arrows
Of outright persecution
This same beatific glance
Also portrays love
In manifestations galore
Of all its faces

REMEMBERING RUDYARD KIPLING

yards
  rods
    miles

days
  weeks
    years

a path stretches on
to hill and hill and hill
beyond what eye can see
over ridge and range

something hidden in the distance
something waiting for you
GO!

ROBINSON JEFFERS IN LINCOLNSHIRE

If Robinson Jeffers
ever lived in Bicker Fen,
after deserting Carmel Bay,
he would find no stones
to press his dreams
of eternity.

In wonder he would view
smoky, grey fog
streaming across the fens
like theater curtains
introducing new scenes.

The flat, green lands
washed by brisk winds
straight from the North Sea,
undeterred by hill or tree,
bounding along
unfettered by predators
whose limiting bonds
might ameliorate
this harsh tribute
to nature's will.

RUINS OF GLASTONBURY ABBEY

grey stones
set in routine patterns
remnants of better days
when walls stood firm
when faith sustained each mind
When love sustained each heart
thorn trees still bloom
just as once they did
after St. Joseph's staff
reached these dense oak shores
then blossomed into seasons
celebrated as Camelot

grey stones
laid in perfect bond
course after course
in honor of the sacred place
peopled by those devout
whose lives were spent
in ceaseless pattern and routine
set down in precious rules
too, founded on that same
faith and love still known
in midst of grassy growth
so fecund in the spring
to submerge grey stones
in soft turf blankets

but still the grey stones lie
in their ancient dignity

Loren N. Horton

SCENES OF SWALEDALE

Dry stone walls
Cross the gorse-carpeted fells
In geometric patterns
Dividing lines become
Fences laid by hands
Fitted with care
Placed precisely
Tighter than tree bark
Starkly grey
Far removed from yew

Hydra-headed tributaries
Gills and becks
Gurgle through the heath
Later to join
River on their way
Dividing dale from dale
But each its own universe

Echoes of prior seasons
Resonate down the valleys
In pale imitation
Of poetic halls of time

Hedge-lined paths
Become romances of nature
Bearing treasures
Brighter than the dawn

Footpaths meander
Through spring water
meadows
Interrupted by stiles
Cluttered with leaves
Lying broken in despair
Reprising last summer

Sheep huddle closely
Rumps against the stone walls
Mutely thankful
for rude shelter
That breaks the force
Of chill winds

Dusty green moors
Undulate beneath cloud shadows
Slopes spare of trees
Wind keening down Buttertubs Pass
Past ridges strewn
With bracken

Chill winter winds
Receive enhancement
From hardy storms
Stirring up the North Sea

Overpowering the scene
Dry stone walls
Fitted with care
Placed precisely
Tighter than tree bark
Contrast to tamed boxwood
Grey lines
Running straight up the fells
Creating chess board scenes
Contrasting with the grassy meadows
Recalling crafts of early times
When pride of work
Was always on display
Rewarded with approving nods

SCENES OF CORNWALL

Pirates dance
	to the ballads of St. Agnes Bay

Rainbows arch over St. Agnes Bay
	brilliant against the metal sky

Trees in Cornwall
	bend away
	from the wind of Land's End

Waves crash
	on the rocks
	beneath John O'Groats

The sky is smeared
	with raindrops coming
	straight from Newfoundland
	spotting the grey rocks
	muting the haunted tones
	of wails
	lost souls of ships
	smashing their prows
	on imaginary gates of Hell

Black flowers of hate
	from Hades

Bottomless cup
	out of which
	you drink and drink
	yet the cup
	is always full

Loren N. Horton

A VIEW AT SCARBOROUGH

That heaving mass of grey
slashing against the seawall,
showering a silver spray,
vomiting forth deceptive froth.

Such brilliant cold,
lighted by stars that sparkle
like chips of Arctic ice,
mist and fog make films
which curtain our view.

Chilled, frozen sea,
forming repetitively
those spirit veils of foam
on each stretch of shingle,
creating patterned shelves,
assaulted by the sea
in relentless charge.

Across the North Sea
unseen but sensed,
that shore of Jutland
beckoning the boats
of hereditary fishermen.

YORKSHIRE MOORS

wastelands of the moors
reaching past the view of eye
undulating like the sea
descending to bracken
creating dangerous bogs
interrupted by occasional copse
not elevated to folly
nor trained into hedge

stretching into darkness
rarely brightened by sun
recalled in myriad novels
glorified as scented heather
haunted shadows drift across
created by wind-blown clouds
drifting in and out of sight
casting unintended gloom

open to the daring hiker
walking briskly on the way
cautioned to keep to paths
avoiding hidden hazards

Yorkshire moors stretch on
in memory and reality
impressive in their breadth
grandeur of an untamed sort

Loren N. Horton

Many Things

BEYOND LABRADOR

What lies beyond
that distant range
of misty ridges ?

When framed
by leafless branches,
it seems to be
so haunted.

Chill fills the air
rising from
the frozen river,
its own flow halted
by winter's power.

BEETHOVEN'S MUSIC

When Beethoven's music
Is played badly
The offense is doubly bad
Because of the sublime possibilities
Inherent in the music itself
Beethoven's compositions
Are exciting
But dynamic changes
For no apparent reasons
Destroys the beauty
Contained in the score itself

ADVENTURE

We went wading in the Grand River
It was an exciting change
From the usual wiener roast
In the timber north of the school
This year our teacher
Loaded us all in his old coupe
And took us on an adventure
For the last day of school
He drove us all the way
To where the Grand River
Made a lazy, sweeping horseshoe bend
Just before O'Grady Corner
Near the Mormon graves

We rolled up our pants legs
And we waded on the smooth bottom
Layered alternately
With sand or wash gravel
The water wasn't really very deep
But to us it seemed like courting danger
The river was quite shallow
But we were still small
The current flowed slowly
And the water was clear and cool
As yet unpolluted and unspoiled
Our picnic on the river bank
Tasted like ambrosia
Everything tasted better
Even though it was just the same
The usual wieners and marshmallows
Roasted over the open fire
And eaten directly off the sticks
Cut from a nearby willow tree

Loren N. Horton

Because we were so far from home
At least four miles away
It seemed to all of us
As if we had crossed the continent
With Lewis and Clark

With full stomachs and contented minds
We loaded back into the old coupe
And the teacher drove us home

BRIDGES

smudged edges
indistinct
against the cast iron
of beams and girders
elongated spans
and swelling arches
soaring
over the currents
above the tides and floods
matching the bowl of sky
reflecting the shadows
of hugging hills
quivering
before gale-force winds
marvels of engineering
triumphs of technology
glorious prizes
of Man and Nature
in unifying force

© Michael W. Lemberger

CHAMBER SINGERS IN CONCERT

How mesmerizing
the rise and fall
of conductor's baton;
producing gorgeous sounds
from many throats,
obedient to note and time.

How penetrating
the music and voices
of chorus blends;
enhancing ear and soul
through many tones,
bringing joy to people.

How inspiring
the sight and sound
of this melding group;
filling hall and mind
with music pure,
another glorious performance.

CHAMBER SINGERS OF IOWA CITY

Beautiful tones
Cast aloft
In planned abandon
Skimming brightly
Across space
Between stage
And audience
Notes crafted
By composers now dead
Performed by singers
Still in flush of life

These songs break forth
On a pleasant afternoon
Spent calming the nerves
And inspiring the spirit

A CLOD

A clod
Lies motionless
Amidst its fellow clods
Drying in the vivid sunlight
Wrenched from the topsoil
By the harsh action
Of the mould-board blade
As it ripped through the surface
Of rich loam

This clod
Now so grey and crumbly
Once sported a jet body
Which adhered dependently
To its nearest neighbors
Broken apart
In alligatoring cracks
As moisture disappeared
And crust formed

What future
For this clod
Soon to disintegrate
Into a pile of dust
Arid until the next rain
But feeling
No human emotion
In the process

COLLECTIONS

Sometimes
I pick up a stone
A shell
A leaf
Sometimes
I pick a flower

These things
Are not detritus
Of a careless soul

They are collections
Set in ordered rows
To become exhibits
Catalogued
By those same hands

Gleaned objects
Now artifacts of my
Treasure

The Colours of the Earth

© Michael W. Lemberger

COLORADO LANDSCAPE

Devastating avalanche
Tumbling landslide
Grey rocks split and shattered
Temper tantrum on a mountain side
Reflection of blackened clouds
Cascade of geological might
Punctuated by bottomless fissures

Angry, roaring waterfall
Cascade of chilled torrent
Cataract sending spray in fans
Meltwater from frigid peaks
Unorthodox glacial masks
Rejected echoes down the valley
True cadenza of bass tones

Father Time
In liaison
With Mother Nature

COMMENT

There is a twitch
I know not where to go
Or what to do
These people flog me with a racking laugh
Oh, these are not the legatees
Of Rimbaud and Verlaine
The sun that gleams and burnishes
Now flickers in the shade
Shield my eyes
With my arm
Tear not the final cup from me
If indeed I thirst
There is no helper here
Sparkling jewels rim the dungeon
But how am I to reach
So high
When hands and hands are clutching me
They level
And in doing so the piling slips
Having no bedrock
To soon be all submerged
In the sucking sands

DAYS

Days come
Days go
Days pass by
Days end
Days follow nights
Days bring sun
        or clouds
        or rain
        or snow
Days are warm or cold
Days are welcomed
        or feared
Days fill our lives

DENVER UNION STATION

nothing surpasses
sombre faces
on wooden benches
people waiting
to board trains
bound
for somewhere else
some destination
that will bring smiles
or tears
all the waiting
will be a memory
wooden benches
relegated
to the pockets of memory
perhaps retrieved
in boring recollections
recited again
and again
to patient relatives
and friends

DREAM SCENE

I have a dream
No, not Martin Luther King, Jr.'s dream
Although that is an admirable dream
My dream recurs
Not every night
But often enough to be noticeable
It concerns floods
And movement
From one side of a river
To the other
I am stranded on the south bank
I need to get across
Even if I do not know
Any great attraction
On the north bank
Those flooded, brown waters roll along
Just like William Warfield's "Old Man River"
Decades ago
Why do I keep having this same dream
Over and over again ?
In between times I have other dreams
Mostly I do not remember them
In any clear detail
But the broad floodplain
Of this particular river
Not matching real geography
Comes back in detail
Along with an urgency
To get to the other side

Not, I sincerely hope,
For the same reasons
Comedians attribute to chickens
I would not want my dream
To be trivialized in such a way
I simply want an explanation
Of why this dream
Repeats, repeats
Without a satisfying conclusion

Can you help me?

DIRECTIONS

We went down the road.
Where exactly is down?
Buildings burn down.
Buildings also burn up.
Directions seem to be essential,
        but the meaning is vague.
Downtown might mean south.
Uptown might mean north.
Both can mean something else.
In and out --
Up and down --
Left and right --
Directions to
        we know not what!

DREAM SKETCHBOOK

Echoes of prior seasons
Resonating down the halls of time
Romances of nature
Bearing treasures
Brighter than the dawn

Studies of north and south
Also directions of the sun
Rising and setting
Sketches of a nether land
Sense of mystery

Fragments of early thoughts
Accumulated within the mind
Courtesy lent to latter days
Elemental comforts
Blended in perfect awe

EARLY HOURS

Who is first ?
Probably the cafe
Catering to the addicts
Satiating demand for coffee
Maybe the school
Opened for music and sports
Before the stampede to classes
Certainly not the bank
Bankers are famous in folklore
For shortened schedules
Never the library
Closed to readers
Lighted for staff
Re-shelving returned books
What about stores ?
Nothing uniform there
Some early, some late
Necessitating a check
In telephone directory
Or morning newspaper

As the sun rises
Activities burgeon
Our town is alive again

Loren N. Horton

EINSTEIN'S THEORY

There is a time that tries men's souls
There is the time that just marches on
While other time stands still

There is time that goes by
Other times have come
While yet another time is ripe

Time is measured
In many ways
By clocks and sundials
An hourglass
Or calendar

Time spent
Time lost
Time wasted by idle hands

Most of all
One must know
When it's time to go

EMOTIONS

echoes
sounds of gladness
pealing across
the nether roads
of wondrous lands

echoes
sounds
lands
coupled in torment
with gladness
and with grief

AN EXERCISE IN PLAGIARISM

Wishes and dreams
Like intentions and goals
Pave the way to change
Whether real or imagined

But change
Is not always progress
As seen in the eyes
Of all beholders

What measuring stick to use
To come to these conclusions ?
That miracle of life -
The human mind

FASTEN

For someone unfamiliar
With the English language
"Fasten" might be related
To the matter of speed

Should we pronounce
The "T" or let it be?

Or perhaps
It is the number
Following nine ?

Is the definition
Clear from the syllables?

Oh, the tribulations!
Decisions -- choices!
A better course might be
Just to say "attach"
        or "clip"
        or "snap"

Loren N. Horton

FAMILY BURYING GROUND

slate
spalling in sheets
like pages from old books
sandstone
crumbling in tiny grains
like snow flakes in a breeze
limestone
weathering in soft cavities
like soap smoothed in bath water
marble
disappearing after lost seasons
like diary entries erased by time
granite
lettering so firmly incised
like swirls of indelible ink
epitaphs
symbolizing love now gone
like petal fragments of old bouquets

FIRST SIGHT

First sight
Of the Front Range
After miles
And miles
Of Great Plains
Is always
Alarming
To first-time viewers
Is it a bank
Of low-lying clouds
That smudges
The horizon ?
A distant storm
Gathering in the West ?
Flatland eyes
Cannot encompass
Such grandeur
Until the chill breeze
From the snow pack
Caresses
Their startled faces
Shadows on the rocks
Blend
In mutability
Until the body
Joins the mind
When arid plains
Meet sheer wall
And reality resumes

GHOST DANCERS

Fearsome ghosts of other times
Hiding along the cracks, the seams
On the lines
That mark the thin places

Ignore the oaks
With hanging dream catchers
Bony out-thrusts
No longer green
But greyed from winter's frost

Ghost dancers from Wounded Knee
Transplanted to Loki's Grove
Transfixed in mind and eye

GIGANTIC OPPOSITES

From chaos comes order?
From experiment comes tradition?
From many, we find the one?

How many wars have spilled our blood
        in useless quest for power?

How many battles must be fought
        for gruesome piles of death?

Soldiers march and fight and die
        in futile, blinded strife

What vision then anticipates
        that quiet stillness - peace?

Come now, liturgy, for those souls,
Lost in mindless war.
A fresh litany for newborn peace.

Dona Nobis Pacem!

THE GLORIOUS 4TH AT THE COUNTY SEAT

Crowded park
Convening place
Grassy expanse
Covered with thinly clad bodies
Together in purpose

Flashes
Flicker in the night sky
Arching high
Disappearing
In scattered bits
Confetti fluttering down
Curtain dropped
To visible horizon
Bombast
Starbursts
Bright lights
Crisscrossing the ebony sky
Unexpected patterns
In colors
So seldom seen
In rapidly closing darkness

Remaining notes
Of Sousa and King
Gently droning
Just beneath the
Explosive crashes
Of simulated cannon fire
Stench of gun powder
Exploded with each
Cartridge

Evening closure
After humid summer day
Gathering
Family, friends, neighbors
In joyous reunion
To celebrate
A birthday
That never was

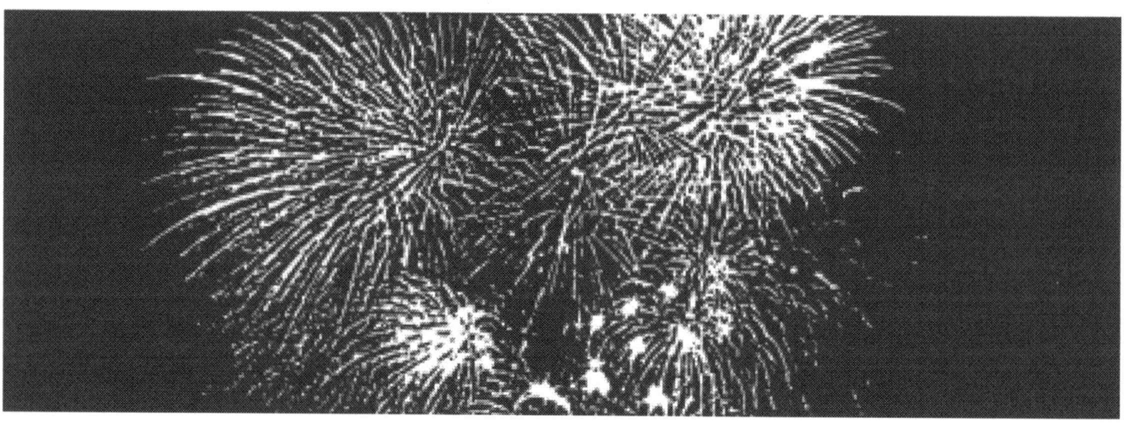

A GROUCHY MAN

"I am grim"
his expression said,
without the need for words.

His frown was stern,
the furrows deep;
while gravity drew
his mouth towards his jaw.

There was no way
to cheer him up;
his course was set
on route to be forlorn.

It only mattered
when his mood
might lighten like the dawn;
when wrinkles smooth
and smile appear
to re-create some joy.

We hope that with
the coming day
his happiness can grow;
while with each passing
moment
his gloom will disappear.

LOVING GLANCES

Cow-eyed youth
Doe-eyed maid
Such glances
Happen in Shropshire
Worthy of note
By Housman

We must admit
Identical glances
Happen in other places
With frequency
And regularity
As does the rising sun

Sometimes noted
As sheep's-eyes
Making sheep's eyes
Being a common expression
In rural Ohio

HOLDING EVELYN

What is this
I'm holding in my arms ?

A small set of bones
covered
with appropriate flesh.

One tiny punctuation mark
crinkles in smile
or serves to communicate
displeasure, need of food.

Five tiny fingers
curl on mother's hand.

Here is a new person
making her way in the world.

May I introduce Evelyn.

SWEET SCENT OF FRESH CUT GRASS

Sweet scent of fresh cut grass
pervades the humid air.

Bees swim to morning glory blossoms.

Butterflies lightly touch milkweed.

A faint, sour smell of sweat
cuts through this daydream
bringing reality check
sending us back to the hayfield

HOLIDAY SEASON

Holidays do not begin
until the waits
have made their rounds

Puddings hang
in muslin sacks
after "Stir up" collect

Greens are hung

Anticipation
grips the hearts
of old and young

THANKSGIVING

Think about the word!
"Thanksgiving".
Is it mainly
giving thanks ?
Or is it
Thanks *for* giving ?

Who is giving what
to whom?
The word rolls glibly
off the tongue;
very little mesh
between the word
and mind.
Not so much
an unbelief
as
suspended thought.

LINES INSPIRED BY AGGRAVATION

Once upon a time
I had to travel
As a part of my work
This often meant
Returning home
Very late at night
My issued state vehicle
Contained only an AM radio
Which offered two choices
Of programs after 10:00 P.M.
Many call-in talk shows
Allowed ignorance
To be distributed widely
Alternative programs
Featured radio evangelists
Of every ilk and type
I always chose to listen
To the radio evangelists
My favorite was The Reverend Ike
Who never preached
He simply asked for donations
In return he offered
Pieces of prayer cloth
One of his testimonials
Avowed that her piece of prayer cloth
Was effective
Because the very next Tuesday
The Lord blessed her with a Buick
Of course that really topped
Any call-in talk show

MEMORIES

We have freed our thoughts
To roam through the past

We can recall
The gentle, green hills
Of spring
Newly clothed at dawn
In soft, velvety robes

We linger a while
In the bright sunlight
Of summer heat

All too soon
Maple leaves turn gold
And crimson in the frost
Of autumn's grip
To merge with dusk
Grown cold
While winter winds
And snow sweeps down
To cover the sleeping earth
With crystallin drifts

So it is with life
From seasons of our youth
Through births and deaths
From morning, noon, and night
To days and months and years
Grown mellow in our sight

Now we free our thoughts
To float pleasantly
Through the past

MEMORIES OF CARMEL BAY

Sounds come back to me at night
In my restless sleep

Relentless pulse of surf
Faded into calm
Rushing into roar
Shattered on sand
Grained on surface

Water sparkles in sunlight
Water glistens in moonlight

Forecast of uneven shores
Edges of events to come
Memories return at will

NOISE

sounds wash over me
sounds buffet my skin
alternating, dinning,
throbbing
undercurrent of force
replacing all options
scattering the pages
like dry leaves
in an autumn whirlwind
sensory perceptions
overwhelm

MYRON'S POND

Cattail reeds grow rank
Along the muddy edges
Of the shallow pond

Green grasses extend
Up the surrounding slope
Broken by the tall growth
Of a single willow tree

An occasional bullhead
Breaks the water's surface
Producing a dance of ripples

Reflections sparkle in sunlight
Brightening this summer view

Loren N. Horton

MY UNCLE'S SAW MILL

blade
hard as a miser's heart
teeth
sharp as a gossip's tongue
whine
unearthly as a banshee's wail

powered by water
pouring through the race
or steam
pressured in the reddened
boiler
later dependent on fossil fuel
internal combustion engine

sustenance obtained
from denuded slopes
not wasting time
or energy
on effeminate cottonwoods
biting powerfully
into mature oaks
and walnuts
bringing forth
in agonizing birth
serrated boards
rough surfaced
like the kiss of coarse
blankets
leaving piles of waste
misnomered dust
eager for the fire
or leisurely decomposition
into rich loam

cycle of birth and death
furnishing nourishment
for future generations
of oak and walnut
standing lofty
in groves and copses
yearning for retired age
anthropomorphism
gives them hope
of living out their lives
in solitude and safety
immune
from human depredation

how frightening the sound
of axe and crosscut
always lurking on the edge
searching
for more sustenance
then to be fed
to blade and teeth
desecration repeated

THE MISSISSIPPI RIVER

Great "Father of Waters"
Who, according to Charles Dickens
Thanks to God
Has no sons
But does have glorious views
Of sunsets
Over the limestone bluffs
Which fortify
The flood plain's western verge

Meandering channels
Dividing sandbars
From willow-covered islands
That gradually eat away
At shallow banks
Supporting miniature cottonwoods
The muddy waters
Clogged with sediment
That formerly graced
An upstream field
This river
Winds a silver path
Towards its chosen goal

Brilliant at sunset
Equally magnificent at dawn
When sunlight peeps
Over the tree-fenced horizon
Challenging in flood time
Pacific in the summer heat
Never to be ignored
A ribbon of beauty
Slicing across the land
Dividing a continent

OLD HIGHWAY 34 WEST OF THAYER

Crumbled asphalt edges
Remnant of arterial highway
Once the favored route
Of travelling families

No longer used
For intended purpose
Discarded, abandoned
Left to shrivel away

Detritus of modern time
Soon to be overgrown
Pigweeds peeping through cracks
Paint faded by sun and frost

Grey ribbon wandering
Aimlessly within a wall of brush
Visible only to the knowing eye
Glancing from a distant car

AN OPINION

Grey
is the forgotten color.
It brings back memories
of the times of sadness.
Slate grey
does not inspire joy.
A rain-laden horizon
conjures up visions
of leaden grey.
Metallic grey
may remind us of battleships and war.
The awe-inspiring grey
of a wolf's eye
brings a tingle of fear.
Unburnished armor
fades from silver to grey.
Is it dim from disuse
or defeat ?
Think of grey
in neutral terms,
taking its rightful place
in the spectrum of colors.

PATRIOTISM

une roi, une loi, une foi
ein volk, ein reich, ein fuhrer
L'etat c'est moi
Dieu et mon droit
e pluribus unum
dulce et decorum est pro patria more

human efforts
to impose order

specious reasoning

PERPETUAL MOTION

Movement, movement
Traffic, people
Trash blowing across streets
Wind holding flags at attention
Banners snapping at right angles
Trees bending in a breeze
Even the sparrows dart past
Restless fingers, eyes, lips
Gadgets multiplying
Television "ads" just fleeting glimpses

Repose seems a forgotten cause
Ease lost in motion
Movement, movement
Everlasting movement

PHILOSOPHY

What is this wispy thought
drifting so ephemerally
through the recesses
of my brain ?

What is this cloudy idea
floating so lightly
through the crannies
of my brain ?

Can it be
that I have found
the answer to my quest ?

Can it be
that future days
will be a shining time ?

Bring to present scenes
no problems or desires
that cannot be endured.

PRAISE

Words of men
Deeds of men
How reverent they can be
When spread with love
And kindness

Elegiac hymns
Exalted in sonority
How majestic they can be
When sung with joy
And gladness

PRIDE

never make a deliberate
attempt
to be sardonic
even when it seems
to come so naturally

it will show up
in looks askance
across some crowded room
vainglorious posturing

expository sense
of raw conceit
results in arrogance
waxing strong
riding roughshod
over themes of mercy
and humility

do not forget
the level place
in which we find
our commonweal

PRIMITIVE CAMPGROUND

Whey-faced ridge
melts into shadow.

Moonlight brightens the crest,
absorbs the blue silhouette;
very like a watercolor,
muted, subdued, vague.

Cool wind whips branches,
scatters twigs
into abstract patterns.

Cast iron earth
emerges fully formed
from alien smelters.

Erratic glacial stones
litter the promenade,
obstacles to sleep
and ambulatory ease.

Weekends, vacations,
break monotonous routines,
provide needed rest.

A QUESTION

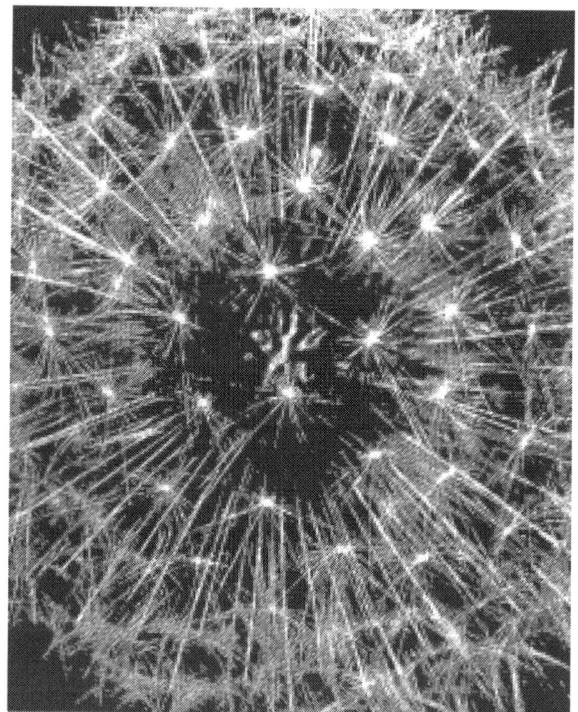
© Michael W. Lemberger

What is that small, green thing
protruding from the crack
in the sidewalk ?
Is it a native wild flower,
soon to bloom
in breathtaking beauty ?
Or is it a weed ?
Who decided
which is weed
and which is flower ?
Dandelions are a puzzle.
Lovely yellow blossoms,
but persecuted mercilessly
by suburban lawn owners.

What if someone prefers
a dandelion to a violet ?
Labelling plants is arbitrary.
Someone made a rule
without asking me.

We ponder questions,
decided whether that sidewalk
is made of cement or concrete.
Just what is the difference ?
One is raw material,
the other manufactured.
Does the difference matter ?

I'll continue to ponder
that small, green thing
protruding from the crack
in the cement or concrete sidewalk,
and hope it live to bloom,
whether weed or flower.

Loren N. Horton

REFLECTIONS

amethyst, topaz, garnet
jewels of highest prize
colors of brightest hue
dazzling glimmer of facets
no somber pall cast down

gemstones of highest worth
glittering against velvet cloth
dramatic flare in shining light
brittle texture showing forth
no dimming, flattened form

THE RETREAT

This old man
simple
thoughtful enough
attended a Retreat

Participated
in unobtrusive ways
held the gentle story-prayers
close to his reason
and he found them to be good

Listened closely
even took a few notes
things to be remembered
recalled later
in times of need

Gradually adapted
to the uncomfortable chairs
to the closeness
of the adjacent people

This old man
came away
at the end of the day
with renewed hope
and with respect
for the joys of solitude

Was this Retreat
a success?

A RORSCHACH DREAM

"In the bleak mid-winter . . .
earth stood hard as iron . . ."
memories of Christina Rosetti
Pre-Raphaelite heroine

White-veiled hills and slopes
stark and barren trees
trees stretching skeletal
branches
in search of nourishing sun

Sheets of suffocating fog
slip between shelves of
brightening layers of light
in dimming distance

This view from hovering hill
brings thoughts of immortality

SEA VIEW

an extraordinary view
this vast span
of sparkling water
covered with little flurries
of white foam
appearing much like
bunches of lace
on a blue dress

strands of weeds
loop across the waves
on their endless journey

a cool wind
sends coils of mist
to dampen the buff sand

SENSES

Plum thicket, grape arbor
Crab apple tree, currant bushes
Rhubarb row, hazelnut brush
Shooting asparagus stalks
Soft plop of falling walnuts
Pungent smell of hog manure
Quiet cluck of Barred Rock chickens
Crawling flocks of box elder bugs
Chatter of a pair of house wrens
Rustle of trembling cottonwood leaves
Nodding hollyhock ranks
Shade of morning glory vines
Scent of purple lilacs
Creaking of maple branches

Our senses retain the memories
Of childhood

SHIELDS

buffalo-hide shield
once protection
for a Kiowa soldier

rounded and stretched
hardened by sweat
rain and snow

dripping fringe
of softened deer-hide
whitened by days
bleached by sunlight

hammered-iron shield
once protection
for a Crusader knight

long and heavy
polished by grooms
whetted and wrought

displaying cross
of crimson enamel
faded by days
bleached by sunlight

shields of other times
kept danger in abeyance

SONORITY

Sonority claims its place
Amidst the clamor
And the subtleties
Bringing into place
A uniformity of sound
That alternately
Blasts the ears
Or soothes the nerves
But always keeps engaged
The mind
The soul
Without attempts to blur
The swelling of the sounds
In broad array

STORY

When
The last word has been spoken
the last stanza written
The last note played

When
That last ray of sunlight fades
The scent of lilacs dwindles

When
The time has come
To pass into the next room
One door shuts, locks

Another door opens
Life takes a turn
And night takes over
Windows are darkened by clouds
Or lighted by stars

Turn the page
Begin another chapter
For the book continues
Or
The story begins again

**STROLLING IN
THE RAIN**

One day last week
I walked in the rain
Going nowhere in particular

The rain drops
Scattered on my hair and face
Spotted the lenses
Of my glasses

Those same drops of rain
Continued their descent
Fell to surface
On the sidewalk squares
There to end their journey

I continued to walk
Content in rain and damp
Never hesitating
In my aimless stroll

THIS SEASON

It is the season
Of the glimmering thought
That rises into being
Alone and unrepentant
Yet fired
With all the fervor
And the furor
Of wild surmise
Conclusions
Can await

The coming of the fullness
Arising
And awakening
In the dawn
Of brightness and of light
This idea brings
The fineness of the day
An understanding
Of our lives

TIME

Time
is measured in many ways.

By clocks
with numbered faces,
with hands which mark the hours
and minutes of the days.

By glasses of sand,
relentlessly sifting
ever down until
exhausted of all grains.

By dials
marking shadows
as the sun moves
across the sky.

By jars of water,
patiently dripping
one to another.

Through all these human schemes
timc moves only
at the pace it sets,
never to be rushed
or stopped

TO MUSIC

Magyar themes
used by Liszt
used by Bartok

Romany melodies
used by Dvorak
used by Brahms

These men, mostly
alien to the Danube plain
inspired by music
transformed by beauty

Apotheosis in life

THE TIME TO SLEEP

Illusions
        a disillusioning flight of fancy
Illustrations
        a lightening slash of envy
        disheartening in the mood

Fade
        a silhouette of dusky lines
        shadow passing shadow form
        a feast that fills the mind
        the rush of murky light
        extending through the sky
        this bagatelle
        subsiding in the winds
                of chance

Gaze
        into impending night
        that starry, sparkling sheet
        of ink that blots the sun
        submerged forever
        midst the webs of sleep

THE UNEXPECTED

It's really quite uncomfortable
When a large clump of wet snow
Falling from a nearby eave
Lands on the back of your neck
But it's not just the cold and wet
As a surprise, it's unpleasant
No permanent damage has been done
Clothing will dry out in time
No blood was drawn nor bones broken

Perhaps it's the indignity of the event
And maybe someone else saw it occur
Making the episode a cause for mirth
A remedy for avoiding such a happening
Can only be to stay inside
Where cold, wet snow is just a view

UPTOWN BILL'S SMALL MALL

Serene surroundings
Friendly people
        going about their business
        minding their own business
Some sitting
        in comfortable chairs
Some sitting
        in rickety chairs
This heavy emphasis
        on books
        on food
        on companionship
A place to go
When worldly cares
Begin to press
Too heavily
On mind and shoulder
Refuge
From "The slings and arrows
        of outrageous fortune"

UPTOWN BILL'S SMALL MALL # 2

"When, in disgrace
With fortune and men's eyes",
There is a place to go
That's safe, secure, and calm
Thanks to a man named Tom
It's Uptown Bill's Small Mall

Loren N. Horton

VOCABULARY

has anyone ever investigated
the acme of acne?
or confused the meaning
of nadir and nada?
one of the oddities of language!
how easily the meanings change
with substitution of letters

east and west share three letters
yet directional dichotomy

vocabulary puzzles

WHAT?

From little to big
from small to large
From tiny to huge
From minute to enormous
From infinitesimal to gigantic

Is this the progression moves?

Or is it opposite
Entirely turned around?

Categories exist
In orderly minds
Perhaps we should desist
Let nature take over
Grow freely
While the mind wanders

VARIATIONS ON A PURPLE THEME

the powers of the mind and eye
move in vastly varied sweeps
on themes of just one word
royal color, worn by emperors
Tyrian purple in its brightest glory
faded to muted hues
applied to lavender, lilac, violet, orchid, amethyst
enhanced to deepened shades
applied to magenta, grape, fuchsia, heliotrope
conjuring pleasant memories of sunsets
"When the deep purple falls over sleepy garden walls"
made popular by Artie Shaw
bringing forth nostalgia
when Sir Edward German
wondered "Who'll buy my lavender ?"
inducing hearty laughter when Sheb Wooley sang
about "The Purple People Eater"
Californians swell with pride
at the sight of purple needlegrass, their state grass
wounded soldiers, since 1917, proudly wear the Purple Heart
gardeners work diligently
for purple blooms of pansy, iris, clematis
triangular purple badge of shame in Nazi death camps
for non-conformists, unorthodox worshippers
followers of popular music
knew of The Riders of the Purple sage
and late of Deep Purple, who rock
writers learn to know purple prose
Zane Grey loved to ride, and write, in the purple sage
Wilson Mizner had a hit on broadway

with "The Deep Purple", about urban crime
even 17th century English villagers
sang "Lavender's blue, dilly, dilly"
San Franciscans enjoyed Dave Brubeck
when he played at The Purple Onion
to an enthusiastic audience of Beatnik poets
all of these disparate thoughts
induced by simple mention of just one word, PURPLE
the mind may wander
and fancy may roam free
from such a homespun start

VIEW FROM KEY LARGO

Can that dolphin
be an argonaut,
separated from companions
in the never-ending quest ?

What voyages of spirit
have you known ?
Across, within, around
the mumbling sea
you venture on
in time.

Current's swift caress
belies the chattering sands
on a nearby shelf.

You watery argonaut
can still maintain the glow
enhanced by challenged surf.

VIEW OF NOTHSIS AHN

The mellow breath of wind
Caresses the timbered ridge
Where oak and hickory trees
Grow in affectionate companionship
Each in their turn
Sharing the life-giving sunlight
And the root-sustaining rain

Coverlets of snow drift down
In random patterns spread about
During chilled seasons of the year

That same wind carried sounds
Of melodies composed by leaves
rustling, whispering, trembling
Before the onslaught gale
Stripping all trees of foliage
Leaving only the naked
Underpinnings
Imperfect bark exposed to air
Visible to intrusive view

VIEW OF THE SOUTH RIDGE

A bowl of sky
hangs over a shelf of hills,
like an umbrella warding off
rain.

Brilliant sky glows
transparent
in prisms of bright light.

Hills punctuate the horizon,
fringed with lacy branches,
fan-like against the line of
sky.

Slopes of megalithic stumps,
upright cords of wood,
stand as foundation piers,
remnants of old timber,
long ago victims
of axe and saw.

Loren N. Horton

VIGNETTE FROM THE FLOODS OF 1993

a siege of brawling water
tumbles past the trembling bridge
blocks travel past the brink

floodtide in full tilt
roils with scoured mud
erodes the willowed bank

from heavy upstream rains
swollen channels charged and full
carry away the land's detritus

THE WAR TO END ALL WARS

When last the nightingale sang its melody
In the dooryard behind our home
Sweet tunes on behalf of a late soldier
Now dead on far-off Argonne field
We heard those songs of sadness
Filtered through the damp, night sky
Penetrating every ear and more
Until the hush of sadness finally fell
New words became so commonplace
We knew Verdun, Ypres, Marne, Somme
Newspapers routinely printed many names
Foch, Allenby, Pershing, Joffre, Haig
We knew them all in mind and heart
Casualty lists perused with anxious eye
And even children heard of those awful times
In trenches, mud, those killed by poison gas
That brought dreadful reality to every town
Yet all the promises of new solutions
Came to nothing in the endless talking
That led to treaties vindictive, harsh
Which no one thought would calm the fears
Of men and women encased in boundaries
Drawn in haste to implement ideas
Never based on ethnic realities
Bunching people into new-formed states
Without the thought of reason or desire
Adrift in subterranean streams of blood
That plebiscites can never justify
Seeds of future conflicts and of wars
Containing bloodshed, horrors undreamed
To devastate civilian territories
Batter architecture previously undisturbed

Into rubble stretching across the view
Maimed bodies littered here and there
Left to merge again with earth
And there become at one with nature
Not unexpected at the end of life
But projected much too soon, this death
May we expect this cycle ever to break
And peace descend like fog upon the land
Where human life is revered, protected
Or will Versailles, and Fourteen Points
Recur again, monotonous repetition

WRONG NOTES

Terrifying in its tessitura
Hackneyed in its repetition
Monotonous in its choice of words
Stultifying in its guttural tones

What can be done
To manipulate this song
And make it please the ear ?

Mostly we let it slip by
and hope for better things to come

HAIKU

in spring the primrose
huddles near the earth's warm crust
gold to please the eye

filmy leaves cast shade
all across the pungent loam
bringing cooling ease

bright bands of yellow
met in glorious wingspread
swallowtail in flight

wings that curve in flight
bring night hawks to our retreat
mellow sounds fill ears

breathy, wispy mist
floating in a sea of blue
morning skies in June

morning light appears
burning off the beads of dew
day has come again

Loren N. Horton

oak trees stand aloof
tall sentinels in the wind
stiff at attention

earth mounded in rows
climb the slopes of rich, black soil
fortune of green corn

white-barked birches
leafless against green hillside
sign of coming fall

scudding clouds drift by
chill winds cut across the fields
season change is near

delicious softness
bare toes on newly plowed dirt
farm fields in the spring

earth crumbled away
brown bank along swollen creek
aftermath of flood

soft moss on tree trunks
always on the northern side
nature's true compass

The Colours of the Earth

modest, brown and still
sparrow on a brittle twig
study in repose

groined vaults of grey sky
rolling thunder looms ahead
summer storm is born

sky turns grey at dusk
stillness settles over all
night becomes our world

yellow petals arch
across our view of hillside
create treasured time

flower petals glow
morning light gleams across leaves
calm fills the new air

glittering stars beam
pass along the midnight way
rest in unknown rooms

shades of brown-turned earth
slope away to distant hills
merge in fringe of oaks

Loren N. Horton

a wind blows softly
bending the tall grass eastward
sign of coming rain

flowers picked from day
blooms and stalks joining color
explosion of joy

bronze leaves flutter down
slashed doublet on nature's sleeve
costume sewed by God

primrose huddled low
violet peeking out of moss
season of new life

brown stubble in rows
scattered husks blowing briskly
corn is gathered in

beams of bright sunlight
penetrate the dark corners
bringing joy to earth

blades of damp green grass
glimmer softly at first light
gift of summer rain

ferns huddle densely
by the roots of willow trees
creating moist nests

mellow browning earth
yellow chaff and sharp stubble
autumn comes to rest

ripening seed piles
granaries and cellars full
storage for winter

slanting fingers rest
on nature's misty carpet
golden rays of light

song birds now in flight
softly glide on gentle winds
poems in motion

sunrise marches in
warming leaves uncurled in air
days of greatest joy

awakening nods
acknowledge another day
a greening season

Loren N. Horton

icy water moves
flowing over smooth-faced stones
nature's polish cloth

the lilacs blooming
fragrance fills the sunny air
spirits rise in joy

a lilac's fragrance
a dandelion's shining
signs of blessed spring

into points of red
vivid flowers seem to grow
destiny fulfilled

morning mist rises
veiling each sharper outline
'til sunlight brightens

jade darts quivering
leaves shimmering in sunlight
willow tree in spring

snow falling at night
soft white flakes pile into drifts
Iowa winter

softly it moves by
evening shadow dark and grey
curtain for bright stars

checker plate ovals
pierced in forced repetitions
corn planting in May

SENRYU

ears flapping at will
tongues wagging all through the day
neighborhood news cast

gentle clink of coins
faint rustle of paper bills
bank tellers at work

swiftly we move on
past the garish colored lights
mall crowds on the prowl

brow furrowed in thought
knuckles whitened in despair
student at exams

About the Author

Loren N. Horton was born near Hopeville, Iowa, graduated from Murray High School, and earned his B.A. and M.A. degrees from Iowa State Teachers College (now University of Northern Iowa). He received the Ph.D. degree from The University of Iowa.

Horton taught in secondary schools in Toledo, Cedar Falls, and Davenport, Iowa, and has been an adjunct instructor at several colleges. He retired from the State Historical Society of Iowa as Senior Historian after a 24-year career.

Horton is the author of 88 articles and 46 book reviews. He is the author of 17 books, including *A Richer Dust Concealed, The Narrow Gate, Rarer Gifts Than Gold,* and *Iowa's Proud Heritage*, from PBL Limited. Although his professional career was as a historian, he has written four volumes of poetry and several plays, and is at work on a mystery novel.

Loren Horton and his wife, Carol, live in Iowa City.

6572779R0

Made in the USA
Charleston, SC
09 November 2010